LAURA & NELLIE

The Little House
Chapter Book Collection

The Adventures of Laura & Jack
Pioneer Sisters
Animal Adventures
Laura & Nellie
Christmas Stories
School Days

LAURA & NELLIE

ADAPTED FROM THE **LITTLE HOUSE** BOOKS BY

Laura Ingalls Wilder

Illustrated by Ji-Hyuk Kim

HARPER

An Imprint of HarperCollinsPublishers

Adaptation by Melissa Peterson

Little House® is a trademark of HarperCollins Publishers Inc.

Laura & Nellie
Text adapted from *On the Banks of Plum Creek*, copyright 1937,
1965, Little House Heritage Trust
Illustrations by Ji-Hyuk Kim
Copyright © 1998 by HarperCollins Publishers

Library of Congress Control Number: 2016957949
ISBN 978-0-06-237713-5

Typography by Jenna Stempel
17 18 19 20 21   OPM   10 9 8 7 6 5 4 3 2 1
❖
Revised edition, 2017

Contents

CHAPTER 1
COUNTRY GIRLS

Laura Ingalls never forgot the first time she met Nellie Oleson. It was on Laura's first day of school, when she lived in Minnesota.

Laura and her big sister, Mary, and her little sister, Carrie, lived on a farm with their Ma and Pa and their bulldog, Jack. Living on a farm meant Laura was a country girl.

Laura loved being a country girl. She loved to run out of the house in the morning and see the dew sparkling on the prairie grass.

She loved to wade in the creek where the minnows swam.

She loved to poke a stick at the old crab who lived in the creek and watch him come out snapping his sharp claws. She loved the good smells of hay and earth and wind.

Nellie Oleson was not a country girl. She was a town girl.

When Nellie Oleson first saw Laura, she wrinkled up her nose as though she smelled something bad. She didn't—she was just being snooty. Nellie's father owned a store, and Nellie thought that made her very important.

"Hmph!" sniffed Nellie Oleson, looking Laura and Mary up and down. She looked at their faded dresses and their long legs sticking out from under the hems. She looked at their braids, tied with thread.

"Country girls!" she said.

Laura didn't much like Nellie Oleson,

even if she did have pretty yellow curls tied with big blue ribbons. Nellie's dress was store-bought. It was smooth and white, with little blue flowers all over. Nellie wore shiny black shoes, and her dress was as light and delicate as a spring day. She was pretty as a picture, except for that wrinkled-up nose.

Laura and Mary were barefoot. When the weather was warm, they always went barefoot. They loved the feel of the soft grass and warm dirt beneath their feet. Ma made all their clothes. She bought sturdy red calico for Laura's dresses, and sturdy blue calico for Mary's. Laura and Mary had never had a white dress like Nellie's.

But Laura and Mary were too busy that first day of school to worry much about Nellie Oleson. They had never been to school before, even though Laura was almost eight and Mary was going on nine. Until now, the places they had lived in had been too far away from any town for them to go to school.

They were excited to meet their teacher, Miss Beadle. She let them inside the one-room schoolhouse and showed them where to sit.

Ma had given Laura and Mary a book to study from. But they did not have a slate.

"I will lend you mine," Teacher said. "You cannot learn to write without a slate."

She lifted up the top of her desk and took out a piece of black board. That was the slate. There was a piece of chalk, too, to write on the slate with.

At noon, all the other children went home to eat. Laura and Mary's house on the farm was two and a half miles away. That was too long a walk to go home for dinner. So Laura and Mary took their dinner pail and sat in a shady spot against the schoolhouse. They ate their bread and butter and talked.

"I like school," Mary said.

"So do I," said Laura. "But I don't like that Nellie Oleson that called us country girls."

"We are country girls," Mary pointed out.

"Yes," Laura said proudly. "She needn't wrinkle her nose!"

CHAPTER 2
TOWN GIRL

The very next day, Laura and Mary had to go to Nellie's father's store. Pa had given them a nickel to buy a slate of their own. They must not go on borrowing Teacher's slate, he said.

The morning sun was shining brightly when they climbed the steps of Mr. Oleson's store. Laura blinked a little inside the cool shady building.

A man stood behind the counter. Laura guessed that was Mr. Oleson, the shopkeeper.

She looked around at all the wonderful things on the shelves—pails and pickles and ploughs and a large round yellow cheese. There were dozens of interesting things for sale. Laura would have liked to look at them all.

But suddenly the back door slammed open. In flounced Nellie Oleson. She looked right at Laura and Mary, standing in the doorway in their bare feet.

"Yah! Yah!" shouted a little boy behind Nellie. He was her brother, Willie, and he had teased Laura and Mary at school the day before. He had called them snipes because their dresses were too short. Snipes were birds with funny long legs, and Laura and Mary did look a little like snipes with their legs sticking out beneath the hems of their dresses. But it wasn't nice to be reminded of it.

"Yah! Long-legged snipes!" Willie jeered now.

"Shut up, Willie," said Mr. Oleson.

But Willie did not shut up. He went on saying, "Snipes! Snipes!"

With a little smile on her face, Nellie walked right past Mary and Laura to a tall wooden barrel that stood on the floor. She dug her hands into the pail and came up with two fistfuls of candy.

It was Christmas candy. There were striped pieces, round pieces, pieces like ribbons. There was red and green and white candy. It was beautiful! Nellie stared right at Laura and Mary, as she crammed the beautiful candies into her mouth.

Willie laughed, and grabbed a handful of candy for himself. He shoveled it into his mouth. Neither one of them offered any to Laura or Mary. Not a single piece.

"Nellie!" said Mr. Oleson. "You and Willie go right back out of here!"

But Nellie and Willie ignored him. *Crunch, crunch* went the candy in their mouths. They kept on staring at Mary and Laura.

Mary turned away from them. She told Mr. Oleson she needed a slate and handed him Pa's nickel.

Mr. Oleson gave her the slate. "You'll want a slate pencil, too," he said. "Here it is. One penny."

"They haven't got a penny," Nellie said.

"Well, take it along, and tell your Pa to give me the penny next time he comes to town," said Mr. Oleson.

But Mary said, "No, sir. Thank you." She turned around and so did Laura, and they walked out of the store.

At the door Laura looked back. Nellie made a face at her. Nellie's tongue was streaked red and green from the candy.

Laura and Mary were quiet as they walked

to the schoolhouse. Laura was worried about the slate pencil they needed to buy. She hated to ask Pa for another penny, after he had spent so much on the slate. Then she remembered their Christmas pennies. One year, back in Indian Territory, they had each found a penny in their Christmas stockings. They could use those pennies for slate pencils. And they would buy the pencils at Mr. Beadle's store, not at Mr. Oleson's.

That made Laura feel better. But she kept thinking about Nellie sticking out her red-and-green tongue.

Mary was still thinking about Nellie, too. "My goodness!" she said. "I couldn't be as mean as that Nellie Oleson."

I could, Laura thought. I could be meaner to her than she is to us, if Ma and Pa would let me.

CHAPTER 3
GAMES

There were lots of children at school whom Laura liked very much. She liked Christy Kennedy, who had stiff red braids and a friendly smile. She liked Christy's brother Sandy, even if he did tease her sometimes. She liked Maud and Nettie and Cassie.

At recess Laura and her friends rushed out of the schoolhouse to play games. It should have been fun, playing games out on the prairie in the sun and the wind. But it wasn't.

Every day they had to play the same old game. Nellie Oleson liked ring-around-a-rosy best, so that's what they always played. Everyone else was tired of tired of ring-around-a-rosy. But Nellie always insisted.

Finally Laura had had enough. One day, as soon as they left the schoolhouse for recess, she said, "Let's play Uncle John!"

Uncle John was a great game. The other girls grinned.

"Let's! Let's!" they cried.

Laura reached out to take Christy's hand. Then she felt a flash of pain on either side of her head, and suddenly she was lying flat on the ground. Nellie was scowling down at her.

"I want to play ring-around-a-rosy!" shouted Nellie.

Laura could not believe it. Nellie Oleson

had grabbed her braids and pulled so hard that Laura fell down. Laura's head stung. The other girls stared in horror.

Laura jumped up. She was boiling mad. Her hand flashed out to slap Nellie.

She stopped it just in time. Pa said she must never hit anybody.

"Come on, Laura," said Christy, holding out her hand.

Laura's face felt hot and she could hardly see. She took Christy's hand. The girls formed a circle around Nellie. Nellie tossed her curls and flounced her skirts, happy she'd gotten her own way.

Then Christy began singing, and all the others joined in:

"Uncle John is sick abed.
What shall we send him?"

"No! No!" Nellie screamed. "Ring-around-a-rosy! Or I won't play!" She broke through the ring.

No one went after her.

"All right," said Christy. "You get in the middle, Maud." They started over.

"Uncle John is sick abed.
What shall we send him?
A piece of pie, a piece of cake,
Apple and dumpling!
What shall we send it in?
A golden saucer.
Who shall we send it by?
The governor's daughter.
If the governor's daughter ain't at home,
Who shall we send it by?"

Then all the girls shouted,

17

"By Laura Ingalls!"

Laura stepped into the middle of the ring and they danced around her. They went on playing Uncle John till Teacher rang the bell.

Nellie was in the schoolhouse, crying. She said she was never going to speak to Laura or Christy again.

But the next week she asked all the girls to a party at her house on Saturday afternoon.

She asked Christy and Laura, specially.

CHAPTER 4
TOWN PARTY

Laura and Mary had never been to a party. What would it be like? they wondered.

Ma said it was a pleasant time that friends had together. Laura thought that sounded nice.

After school on Friday Ma washed their dresses and sunbonnets. Saturday morning she ironed them, fresh and crisp.

Laura and Mary bathed that morning, too, instead of that night as they usually did. They put on their fresh, clean dresses.

"You look sweet and pretty as posies," Ma said. She tied on their Sunday hair-ribbons. Mary's were blue and Laura's were red, to match their dresses.

Ma warned them not to lose the ribbons. "Be good girls," she said, "and mind your manners."

They set off down the path. When they came to town, they stopped for Cassie and Christy. Cassie and Christy had never been to a party, either. They all went timidly into Mr. Oleson's store.

"Go right on in!" said Mr. Oleson.

So they went past the candy and pickles and ploughs, to the back door of the store.

The door opened. There stood Nellie, all dressed up. Behind her was Mrs. Oleson, asking them in.

Laura had never seen such a fine room.

She felt very shy. She could hardly say, "Good afternoon, Mrs. Oleson."

The whole floor was covered with some kind of rough, heavy cloth. It was brown and green, with red and yellow scrolls all over it.

The walls and the ceiling were smooth boards. There were colored pictures on the walls.

The table and chairs were of a yellow wood that shone like glass. Their legs were perfectly round. Laura's Pa made nice wooden furniture, but he could never get the legs as perfectly round as that. Only a machine could do that.

"Go into the bedroom, girls, and leave your bonnets," said Mrs. Oleson in her company voice.

The bedroom furniture was made of shiny wood, too. There were glass windows in both rooms, with white lace curtains.

Soon all the guests had arrived. Mrs. Oleson's skirts rustled among them. Laura could have just stood there and looked at all the fine things, but Mrs. Oleson said, "Now, Nellie, bring out your playthings."

Nellie frowned. "They can play with Willie's playthings," she said.

"They can't ride on my velocipede!" Willie shouted.

"Well, they can play with your Noah's ark and your soldiers," snapped Nellie.

Mrs. Oleson told Willie to be quiet. She brought out his Noah's ark.

Laura thought it was the most wonderful thing she had ever seen. It was filled with tiny wooden animals—zebras and elephants and tigers and horses. All the girls knelt down and squealed and laughed over it.

And there were two whole armies of tin soldiers. One army was bright blue, and the

other was bright red.

There was a jumping-jack. He wore striped paper clothes and a tall pointed cap. His face was painted white with red cheeks and circles around his eyes. He could dance, turn somersaults, and stand on his head with his toe on his nose.

Even the big girls like Mary and Cassie squealed over the animals and the soldiers. They laughed at the jumping-jack until they cried.

Then Nellie pushed into the middle of them all.

"You can look at my doll," she said.

The doll had a china head, with smooth red cheeks and a cherry red mouth. Her eyes were black, and she had wavy black china hair. She had tiny china hands, and tiny china feet in black china shoes.

"Oh!" Laura said. "Oh, what a beautiful

doll! Oh, Nellie, what is her name?"

Nellie tossed her head "She's nothing but an old doll. You wait till you see my wax doll."

She threw the china doll in a drawer. Then she took out a long box and put it on the bed. She opened the lid. All the girls leaned around her to look.

In the box lay a doll that seemed to be alive. Real golden hair lay in soft curls on her little pillow. Her lips were parted, showing two tiny white teeth. Her eyes were closed. The doll was sleeping there in the box.

Nellie lifted her up. The doll's big blue eyes opened wide. She seemed to laugh. Her arms stretched out and she said, "Mamma!"

"She does that when I squeeze her stomach," Nellie said. "Look!"

She punched the doll's stomach hard with her fist. "Mamma!" the doll cried out.

Her dress was made of blue silk. She wore

real petticoats trimmed with ruffles and lace. On her feet were real little blue leather slippers. She was beautiful.

All this time Laura had not said a word. She couldn't. She had never seen anything like this wonderful doll. Without meaning to, her finger reached out toward the blue silk.

"Don't you touch her!" Nellie screeched. "You keep your hands off my doll, Laura Ingalls!"

CHAPTER 5
SWEET CAKE AND SOUR LEMONADE

Nellie clutched the doll to her chest. She turned her back on Laura so that Laura could not see her putting the doll back in the box.

Laura's face burned hot. The other girls did not know what to do. They watched Nellie put the box in a drawer and slam it shut.

Laura sat on a chair. The other girls played with the animals and squeezed the jumping-jack. Nellie's mother came in and asked Laura why she was not playing.

"I would rather sit here, thank you, ma'am," Laura said politely.

"Would you like to look at these?" asked Mrs. Oleson. She laid two books in Laura's lap.

"Thank you, ma'am," said Laura.

Carefully she turned the pages of the books. One was not exactly a book. It was thin and had no covers. It was a little magazine, all for children.

The other was a book with a thick, glossy cover. On the front was a picture of an old woman wearing a pointed hat and riding on a broom. Large letters over her head said:

MOTHER GOOSE

Laura had not known there were such wonderful books in the world. She forgot all about the party. On every page of the book

was a picture and a rhyme, and she could even read some of the rhymes.

Suddenly Mrs. Oleson was speaking to her. "Come, little girl. You mustn't let the others eat all the cake, must you?"

"No, ma'am," Laura said. She laid the book down. Mrs. Oleson led her to a table, where there was a big white cake.

Nellie grabbed a piece of the cake. "I got the biggest piece!" she shouted. The other girls waited quietly while Mrs. Oleson served the cake. She put each piece on a china plate.

Each girl got a piece of cake and a tall glass of something to drink.

"Is your lemonade sweet enough?" Mrs. Oleson asked. So Laura knew that it was lemonade in the glasses. She had never tasted anything like it. At first the lemonade was sweet, but after she ate a bit of her cake, it was sour. But she didn't tell Mrs. Oleson that.

She was careful not to drop one crumb of cake on the tablecloth. She didn't spill a drop of lemonade. She could see that Mary and the other girls were being very careful, too.

Then the delicious cake was gone. It was time to go home. Laura remembered what Ma had told her to say.

"Thank you, Mrs. Oleson. I had a very good time at the party." She thought of Nellie's face, all pinched up when she screamed at Laura not to touch the doll. But to Mrs. Oleson she just smiled politely and said good-bye.

The girls filed through the store. Outside, Christy Kennedy turned to Laura. "I wish you'd slapped that mean Nellie Oleson," she said.

"Oh no! I couldn't!" Laura said. "But

I'm going to get even with her." She looked around. "Shh! Don't let Mary know I said that."

When they got home, Laura and Mary told Ma all about the party. But they didn't tell about how mean Nellie was, or how she had yelled at Laura. They told Ma about the cake, and the lemonade, and the table with the round legs, and the wonderful toys.

Ma looked thoughtful. "We must not accept hospitality without making some in return," she said. "You must ask Nellie Oleson and the others to a party here. I think a week from Saturday."

CHAPTER 6
COUNTRY PARTY

"Will you come to my party?" Laura asked Christy and Maud.

"Will you come to my party?" she asked Nellie Oleson.

Mary asked the big girls. Everyone said they would come—even Nellie.

That Saturday morning the house was especially pretty. The scrubbed floors shone, and Jack was not allowed to come inside. The windows gleamed. The pink-edged curtains were freshly crisp and white.

Laura and Mary made new starry papers for the shelves behind Ma's stove. They used long strips of brown wrapping-paper, folded in a special way. Mary and Laura cut tiny bits out of the folded paper with scissors. When they unfolded the papers, there was a row of stars to hang over the edges of the shelves.

And Ma made vanity cakes. She made them with beaten eggs and white flour. She dropped each little cake into a kettle of sizzling fat. Each one came up bobbing. It floated till it turned itself over, lifting up its honey-brown bottom. Then it swelled underneath till it was round. Ma lifted it out with a fork.

She put every one of the cakes into the pantry. They were for the party.

Laura and Mary and Carrie and Ma were

dressed up and waiting when the guests came walking out from town. Even Jack was neatly brushed. His brown and white fur shone handsomely.

Jack ran with Laura down to the ford, where the creek cut across the road. The guests came laughing and splashing through the sunny water.

All except Nellie. She had to take off her shoes and stockings first. Then she complained that the gravel hurt her feet.

"I don't go barefoot," she sniffed, as if going barefoot was shameful.

She was wearing another new dress. Big new bows stuck out above her golden curls.

"Is that Jack?" Christy asked, pointing at the dog. Everyone patted him and said what a good dog he was.

Everyone except Nellie.

"Go away!" she said. Jack wagged his tail at her politely. "Go away! Don't you touch my dress!"

"Jack wouldn't touch your dress," Laura said.

They went up the path between the blowing grasses and wildflowers. At the house Ma was waiting in the doorway. Mary told her the girls' names one by one. Ma smiled her lovely smile and said hello.

Nellie smoothed the skirt of her pretty new dress. She spoke to Ma. "Of course I didn't wear my best dress to just a country party."

That did it. Laura didn't care if she got punished—she was going to get even with Nellie. Nellie couldn't speak that way to Ma!

Ma only smiled and said, "It's a very pretty dress, Nellie. We're glad you could come."

But Laura was not going to forgive Nellie so easily.

The girls liked the house Pa had built. It was so clean and airy, with a sweet-smelling breeze blowing through.

Everyone climbed the ladder and looked at the attic where Laura and Mary slept. It was one big room as wide as the whole downstairs, and it belonged just to Laura and Mary. That was where they slept, and where they played in winter. None of the other girls had anything like that.

But Nellie asked, "Where are your dolls?"

Laura had one doll, a rag doll named Charlotte. She had had Charlotte ever since she was a tiny girl back in the Big Woods of Wisconsin. Charlotte was old and faded now, but she was still Laura's darling.

There was no way Laura was going to show her beloved Charlotte to Nellie Oleson.

"I don't play with dolls," she said. "I play in the creek."

So they all went outdoors with Jack. Laura showed them all around Pa's farm. They looked at the little chicks by the haystacks. They looked at the green garden rows and the golden wheatfield. Then they ran down the path to play in Plum Creek.

Laura showed them the little footbridge that crossed the creek, and the big willow that dipped its branches into the gurgling water.

Mary and the big girls came down slowly, bringing Carrie to play with. But Laura and Christy and Maud and Nellie went wading in the cool water. They held their skirts above their knees to keep them dry. Around their feet tiny minnows swam.

After a while they climbed back onto the grassy bank and played a game of tag. Then they went wading again.

And that's when Laura thought of a way to get even with Nellie.

A little way down the creek, there was a big flat rock in the water. Laura knew that under that rock there lived a big old crab. Sometimes she poked under his rock with a stick, and he would rush out, snapping his fierce claws. Once she had seen him snap a stick in two with one huge claw.

And not far from his rock, there was a place where the plum trees leaned out from the bank. The water beneath their branches was dark and muddy. Something else lived in that muddy water—something worse than a crab.

Laura looked at Nellie. Yes, that was what she would do. Laura led the girls wading near the old crab's home. He was under his rock, glaring at the noisy girls. Laura could see his angry eyes and browny-green head peeping out.

She crowded Nellie near his rock. Then she kicked a big splash of water onto the stone and she screamed,

"Oo, Nellie! Look out!"

The old crab rushed at Nellie's toes, snapping his claws to nip them.

CHAPTER 7
GETTING EVEN

Nellie shrieked in terror.

"Run! Run!" Laura yelled.

She pushed Christy and Maud back toward the bridge. Then she ran after Nellie. Nellie ran screaming straight into the muddy water under the plum trees.

Laura stopped and looked back at the crab's rock.

"Wait, Nellie," she said. "You stay there."

"Oh, what was it?" Nellie asked. "What

was it? Is he coming?"

She had dropped her skirt, and her pretty new dress hung in the muddy water.

"It's an old crab," Laura told her. "He cuts big sticks in two with his claws. He could cut our toes right off."

Nellie turned pale. "Where is he? Is he coming?"

"You stay there and I'll look." Laura waded back to the rock. The old crab had gone back underneath, but Laura didn't say so. She kept going, and waded all the way to the bridge. Nellie watched her from the muddy water beneath the plum trees.

Slowly Laura waded back toward Nellie. "You can come out now," she said.

Nellie came out into the clean water. She said she didn't like that horrid old creek and wasn't going to play anymore.

She rinsed her muddy skirt in the clear

43

water. Then she tried to wash the mud off her feet.

That was when she started screaming.

Something was stuck to her legs. All over her legs and feet were small brown blobs the color of mud.

The blobs were soft and squishy like mud. But they weren't mud. They were worms.

Once Laura had wandered into that muddy water under the plum thicket, and the mud-brown worms had stuck to her legs. She had yelled and yelled, and when she tried to pull them off, they stretched out long and thin. Laura had to pull very hard until the worms popped off her skin. It had made her feel sick. Pa said the worms were called bloodsuckers. Ma said they were leeches, and doctors used them to heal sick people.

Nellie tried to pick one of the bloodsuckers off her leg. It stuck tight to her skin. She ran

screaming out of the water. Up on the bank she stood kicking her legs, trying to shake off the bloodsuckers. She screamed and screamed.

Laura giggled. Nellie looked so funny kicking first one leg, then the other. Laura laughed so hard she fell on the grass. "Oh look, look!" she shouted. "See Nellie dance!"

All the girls came running. Mary told Laura to pick those bloodsuckers off, but Laura didn't listen. She lay on the grass, rolling with laughter.

"Laura!" Mary said. "You get up and pull those things off, or I'll tell Ma."

Laura sat up, still giggling, and went over to Nellie. She grabbed one of the bloodsuckers and pulled hard. It stretched long, and longer, and longer. All the girls screamed. At last the bloodsucker popped off, and that made the girls scream even louder. One by one Laura pulled the leeches off Nellie's legs.

"I don't like your party!" Nellie sobbed. "I want to go home!"

Ma came hurrying down to the creek to see why they were screaming. She told Nellie not to cry. A few leeches were nothing to cry about. Besides, she said, it was time now for them all to come to the house.

The table was set prettily with Ma's best white cloth. In the center was a blue pitcher full of flowers. The benches were drawn up on either side of the table. Shiny tin cups were full of cold, creamy milk. And Ma's big platter was heaped with golden-brown vanity cakes.

The cakes were rich and crisp. Their insides were hollow. Each one was like a great bubble. The crisp bits melted on the tongue.

The girls ate and ate. They said they had never tasted anything so good, and they asked

Ma what they were.

"Vanity cakes," said Ma. "Because they are all puffed up, like vanity, with nothing solid inside."

There were so many vanity cakes that they ate till they could eat no more. They drank all the cold, sweet milk they could hold. Then the party was over.

All the girls said thank you for the party—all except Nellie. Nellie was still mad.

Laura didn't care. Christy hugged her and whispered, "I never had such a good time! And it just served Nellie right!"

Laura thought of Nellie dancing on the creek bank. Deep down inside her, she smiled.

CHAPTER 8
NELLIE SHOWS OFF

Winter came, and Laura and Mary had to begin wearing shoes. They missed the barefoot days of summer.

After a while it was too cold for Laura and Mary to walk to school. Ma gave them their lessons at home. They hardly ever saw Nellie Oleson anymore. Laura didn't miss her one bit.

But one bright morning Pa said they would take a trip to town. Mary needed new shoes.

Her feet had grown too big for her old shoes, and her toes were pinched. So were Laura's. She could hardly walk without limping.

Pa said Laura could wear Mary's old shoes, but Mary would need a new pair. And for that, they must go to town.

He hitched up the wagon. Ma and Mary and Laura rushed around, getting ready to leave. Everyone climbed into the wagon. The frosty air nipped their noses, but the sun was bright and cheerful.

The horses trotted gaily all the way to town. Pa tied them to the hitching post in front of a store. It wasn't Mr. Oleson's store. This store belonged to Mr. Fitch.

Pa bought flour and sugar. Then he counted his money and bought a pair of shoes for Mary.

The shoes were new and shining on Mary's feet. It wasn't fair that Mary was the oldest, Laura grumbled to herself. Mary's old shoes would always fit Laura, and Laura would never have new shoes.

Then Ma said, "Now, a dress for Laura."

Laura's heart skipped a beat. She raced to the counter where Ma was looking at cloth.

The winter before, Ma had let out every tuck and seam in Laura's winter dress. This winter it was very short. She looked even more like a snipe than she had in her old summer dress. And there were holes in the sleeves where her elbows had gone through. Ma had patched them, and the patches did not show. But still, in that dress Laura felt skimpy and patched.

But she had not dreamed of getting a whole new dress.

"What do you think of this golden-brown flannel, Laura?" asked Ma.

It was beautiful. Laura couldn't say a word.

Mr. Fitch said, "I guarantee it will wear well."

Ma laid some red braid across the golden-brown. She said she might use the braid to trim the collar and cuffs and waistband.

"What do you think, Laura? Would that be pretty?"

"Oh yes, Ma!" Laura's eyes shone. Pa smiled at her.

"Get it, Caroline," he said.

Mr. Fitch measured off the beautiful golden-brown flannel and the red braid.

Then it was Mary's turn. But there was no cloth in Mr. Fitch's store that she liked.

So they all crossed the street to Mr. Oleson's store.

Right away Mary found exactly what she wanted. She chose dark blue flannel with narrow golden braid for the trim.

Mr. Oleson measured it out. Mary and

Laura leaned in close to admire the soft blue flannel.

Then the back door opened, and Nellie Oleson walked in. She was wearing a little fur cape around her shoulders. It was lovely and looked very warm. Her golden curls shone above the soft fur. But her eyes were mean as ever.

"Hello!" she said. She looked at the blue flannel her father was measuring, and sniffed. She said it was all right for country folks. Then she turned to show off her fur. "See what *I* got!"

Laura and Mary couldn't help looking.

"Don't you wish you had a fur cape, Laura?" Nellie asked. "But your Pa couldn't buy you one. Your Pa's not a shopkeeper."

Laura was so angry she could not speak. She ached to slap Nellie, but she knew she must not. All she could do was ignore Nellie.

54

Laura turned her back, and Nellie went away laughing.

Ma was buying warm cloth to make a cloak for Carrie. Pa was buying navy beans and cornmeal and salt and tea. By then it was after noon, and growing colder. They bundled back into the wagon and hurried home.

After dinner Ma opened the store packages so they could all look at the pretty cloth.

"I'll make your dresses as quickly as I can, girls," Ma said. "Because now that Pa is home we'll be going to Sunday school again."

Sunday school! That was exciting news. Laura loved to go to church and sit in Mrs. Tower's Sunday school class. Mrs. Tower was a very nice lady who told them Bible stories. Afterward, it was time for grown-up church. Everyone sang songs, and Reverend Alden gave a sermon.

Laura liked Reverend Alden, with his

warm eyes and friendly smile. But it had been a long time since they had been to church. Pa had gone away for many weeks, to find work back East. Now he was home again, and there was money for new dresses, and they could go to Sunday school. Laura forgot all about Nellie Oleson and her fur cape.

She remembered Nellie on Sunday, though. There she was in church, wearing her lovely cape. She was showing it off to all the other girls, smiling proudly.

Laura remembered what Nellie had said about Pa. She burned hot inside. She knew that hot feeling was wicked. She knew she must forgive Nellie, or she would never be an angel. She thought hard about the pictures of beautiful angels in the big Bible at home. They wore long white nightgowns.

Not one of them wore a fur cape.

CHAPTER 9
SURPRISE

One afternoon Ma said there would be no lessons at home. Instead, they must all take baths and get ready to go to town.

Laura and Mary were surprised. They never took baths in the middle of the week, only on Saturdays. And they never went to town at night.

"There must always be a first time," Ma said.

"But why?" Laura wanted to know. "Why

are we going to town at night?"

"It's a surprise," said Ma. "Now, no more questions."

So they all took baths, and everyone put on her best clothes. There had never been such a scrubbing and scampering. Shoes were brushed, hair was braided, and hair ribbons were tied in perky bows.

Laura and Mary were bursting with questions. They whispered to each other and wondered. What was the surprise?

Even Pa took a bath and put on his Sunday clothes. Then he tucked them all into the wagon and drove away toward town.

The town seemed asleep. The stores were dark as Pa drove past them.

Then Laura exclaimed, "Oh, look at the church! How pretty it is!"

The church was full of light. Light spilled out of all its windows. Laura almost jumped out from under the blankets, even before the wagon stopped moving. She remembered just in time to wait for Pa to stop the horses.

Pa covered the horses with their blankets. Then they all walked into the church together.

Laura's mouth fell open. All the benches were crowded with people. And up in front, there was a tree.

At least, Laura thought it must be a tree. She could see its trunk and branches. But she had never before seen a tree like this.

Where leaves would be in summer, there were streamers of thin green paper. Among them hung little pink sacks of candy.

From the branches hung packages. There were red packages and pink packages and yellow packages, all tied with colored string. Between the packages hung silk scarves, and red mittens, and a pair of new shoes.

Under the tree were all sorts of other

things—a new sled, a crinkly-bright washboard, a churn, a long-handled pitchfork.

Laura was too excited to speak. She squeezed Mary's hand tighter and tighter. What kind of tree *was* that?

Ma smiled Laura. "That is a Christmas tree, girls. Do you think it is pretty?"

They nodded, their eyes wide. They could not take their eyes off that wonderful tree. They had almost forgotten that it was Christmas!

Just then Laura saw the most wonderful thing of all. High up on the tree hung a little fur cape. It was even prettier than Nellie's, and there was a little fur muff to go with it, for keeping your hands warm.

Reverend Alden stood in the front of the church and talked about Christmas. Laura was looking at the tree so hard she could hardly hear him. Then everyone sang a song, but Laura couldn't make a sound.

After the singing, Mr. Tower and Mr. Beadle began taking things off the tree. They read out a name for each package. Mrs. Tower and Miss Beadle gave the package to the person whose name was called.

Everything on that tree was a Christmas present for somebody!

The lamps and voices and even the tree began to whirl in Laura's mind. They whirled faster, noisier, and more excited. Someone gave her a pink bag of candy. Mary had one, too. So did Carrie. There was one for every girl and boy.

Then Mary got a pair of blue mittens. Laura got a red pair.

Ma opened a big package, and there was a warm shawl for her. Pa got a woolly scarf. For Carrie there was a rag doll with a china head. She screamed for joy.

Everywhere there was talking and laughing and papers rustling. Mr. Tower and Mr. Beadle went on shouting names.

The little fur cape and muff still hung on the tree.

Laura wanted them. She wanted to look at them as long as she could. Who would get them? They could not be for Nellie Oleson. She already had a cape.

Laura didn't expect to get anything more. After all, she had already been given mittens and candy! But then Mrs. Tower gave Mary a pretty little book with Bible pictures in it.

Mr. Tower was taking the fur cape and the muff from the tree. He read a name. But Laura couldn't hear it through all the noise.

She lost sight of the cape and muff among all the people. They were gone now.

"Merry Christmas, Laura!" Miss Beadle said. She gave Laura a beautiful little box.

It was made of snow-white china. On its top stood a tiny golden teapot and a tiny golden cup in a golden saucer. Ma said it was a jewel-box. The top of the box lifted off, and inside was a place to keep jewelry.

There had never been such a Christmas as this. The church was filled with so many lamps, so many people, so much noise and laughter and happiness. Laura felt full to bursting, as if that whole big rich Christmas was inside of her.

And then someone said, "These are for you, Laura."

It was the fur cape and muff. Mrs. Tower stood smiling, holding them out to Laura.

"For me?" Laura said. "For me?"

She reached out to touch the warm brown fur. It was silky-soft. She hugged the furs to her chest. She could hardly believe they were hers.

All around her Christmas went on. But Laura knew only the softness of those furs.

People were going home. Carrie was standing on the bench while Ma tied on her hood. Pa and Ma were thanking the Reverend Alden for their shawl and scarf.

The Reverend Alden sat down on the bench. "And does Mary's coat fit?" he asked.

Laura had not noticed Mary's new coat until then. It was dark blue, and it fit Mary perfectly.

"And how does this little girl like her furs?" the Reverend Alden asked, smiling.

He laid the fur cape around her Laura's shoulders and fastened it at the throat. He put the cord of the muff around her neck. Laura put her hands inside the silky muff.

"There!" the Reverend Alden said. "Now my little country girls will be warm when they come to Sunday school."

"What do you say, Laura?" Ma asked.

But the Reverend Alden said, "There is no need. The way her eyes are shining is enough."

Laura could not speak. The golden-brown fur cuddled her neck and hugged her shoulders. The muff came far up her wrists and hid the shortness of her old coat sleeves.

"She's a little brown bird with red trimmings," said the Reverend Alden.

Laura laughed. It was true. Her hair and her coat and her dress and her wonderful furs were brown. Her hood and mittens and the braid on her dress were red.

Laura found her voice. "Thank you, sir," she said to Reverend Alden.

Then they were all going home. Mary was beautiful in her new blue coat. Golden-haired

Carrie was so pretty on Pa's arm. Pa and Ma were smiling happily, and Laura was all gladness.

Mr. and Mrs. Oleson were going home too. Mr. Oleson's arms were full of things, and so were Nellie's and Willie's. Nellie's fur cape was around her shoulders. No wickedness boiled up in Laura now. She only felt glad.

"Merry Christmas, Nellie," Laura said. Nellie stared. Laura walked quietly on, her hands snuggled deep in the soft muff.

If you're done with your chores,
have fun with these

Activities!

MEET LAURA

Laura Ingalls Wilder was born in the Big Woods of Wisconsin on February 7, 1867, to Charles Ingalls and his wife, Caroline.

When Laura was still a baby, Pa and Ma decided to move to a farm near Keytesville, Missouri, and the family lived there about a year. Then they moved to land on the prairie south of Independence, Kansas. After two years in their little house on the prairie, the Ingallses went back to the Big Woods to live in the same house they had left three years earlier.

This time the family remained in the Big Woods for three years. These were the years that Laura wrote about in her first book, *Little House in the Big Woods*.

In the winter of 1874, when Laura was seven, Ma and Pa decided to move west to Minnesota. They found a beautiful farm near Walnut Grove, on the banks of Plum Creek.

The next two years were hard ones for the Ingallses. Swarms of grasshoppers devoured all the crops in the area, and Ma and Pa could not pay off all their debts. The family decided they could no longer keep the farm on Plum Creek, so they moved to Burr Oak, Iowa.

After a year in Iowa, the family returned to Walnut Grove again, and Pa built a house in town and started a butcher shop. Laura was ten years old by then, and she helped earn money for the family by working in the dining room of the hotel in Walnut Grove, babysitting, and running errands.

The family moved only once more, to the little town of De Smet in Dakota Territory. Laura was now twelve and had lived in at least twelve little houses. Laura grew into a young lady in De Smet, and met her husband, Almanzo Wilder, there.

Laura and Almanzo were married in 1885, and their daughter, Rose, was born in December 1886. By the spring of 1890, Laura and Almanzo had endured too many hardships to continue farming in South Dakota. Their house had burned down in 1889, and their second child, a boy, had died before he was a month old.

First, Laura, Almanzo, and Rose went east to Spring Valley, Minnesota, to live with Almanzo's family. About a year later they moved south to Florida. But Laura did not like Florida, and the family returned to De Smet.

In 1894, Laura, Almanzo, and Rose left De Smet for good and settled in Mansfield, Missouri.

When Laura was in her fifties, she began to write down her memories of her childhood, and in 1932, when Laura was 65 years old, *Little House in the Big Woods* was published. It was an immediate success, and Laura was asked to write more books about her life on the frontier.

Laura died on February 10, 1957, three days after her ninetieth birthday, but interest in the Little House books continued to grow. Since their first publication so many years ago, the Little House books have been read by millions of readers all over the world.

The Little House Family Tree

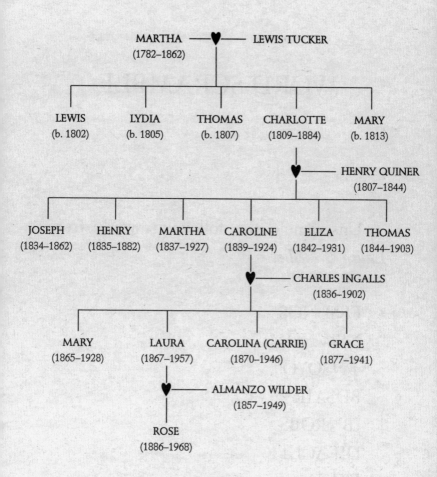

MARTHA ━━♥━━ LEWIS TUCKER
(1782–1862)

LEWIS (b. 1802) LYDIA (b. 1805) THOMAS (b. 1807) CHARLOTTE (1809–1884) MARY (b. 1813)

━━♥━━ HENRY QUINER (1807–1844)

JOSEPH (1834–1862) HENRY (1835–1882) MARTHA (1837–1927) CAROLINE (1839–1924) ELIZA (1842–1931) THOMAS (1844–1903)

━━♥━━ CHARLES INGALLS (1836–1902)

MARY (1865–1928) LAURA (1867–1957) CAROLINA (CARRIE) (1870–1946) GRACE (1877–1941)

━━♥━━ ALMANZO WILDER (1857–1949)

ROSE (1886–1968)

WORD SCRAMBLE

Unscramble the following words from *Laura & Nellie*!

ESSLNOS

NSWNOMI

TNSOYO

BDSAIR

IBNROBS

DIEACLTE

KHCAL

OBDRA

LSCOOH

AHTLORTEC

HPEPESEKOR

ARLBRE

ABFUIUELT

NCCHUR

CEKILN

EFIDSWRLWLO

RREENEVD

ESRCES

SOSEIP

RCHHUC

WORD SEARCH

Find the following words from *Laura & Nellie* in the puzzle below!

PLEASANT	PETTICOAT	MUDDY
PICTURES	RHYME	THICKET
ELEPHANT	PENNY	LEECH
PLAYTHING	PARTY	NELLIE
FLANNEL	BAREFOOT	SNIPES
SOLDIERS	DARLING	COUNTRY
LEMONADE	CRAB	

```
A S O B N Y C R A B E S N
M C I A G L E E C H P B G
F X E R S N I A Y F L I S
H D I E P I C T U R E S O
S P C F E K R G N F A I L
L E M O N A D E A G S T D
K T L O N D L N F O A B I
C T F T Y Z E F L A N N E
O I O E L E P H A N T J R
U C N L H C L T N E S G S
N O E E D G A P N O D S J
T A L P A R Y N E L A N X
R T L E R K T H L X D I M
Y M I P L R H Y M E L P U
T H E E T H I C K E T E D
X D A R L I N G H J E S D
L M E O P M G Z P A R T Y
```

ANSWER KEY

Word Scramble:

LESSONS	SCHOOL
MINNOWS	CHARLOTTE
SNOOTY	SHOPKEEPER
BRAIDS	BARREL
RIBBONS	BEAUTIFUL
DELICATE	CRUNCH
CHALK	NICKEL
BOARD	WILDFLOWERS

REVEREND   POSIES

RECESS   CHURCH

Word Search:

```
A  S  O  B  N  Y  C  R  A  B  E  S  N
M  C  I  A  G  L  E  E  C  H  P  B  G
F  X  E  R  S  N  I  A  Y  F  L  I  S
H  D  I  E  P  I  C  T  U  R  E  S  O
S  P  C  F  E  K  R  G  N  F  A  I  L
L  E  M  O  N  A  D  E  A  G  S  A  D
K  T  L  O  N  D  L  N  F  O  A  B  I
C  T  F  T  Y  Z  E  F  L  A  N  N  E
O  I  O  E  L  E  P  H  A  N  T  J  R
U  C  N  L  H  C  L  T  N  E  S  G  S
N  O  E  E  D  G  A  P  N  O  D  S  J
T  A  L  P  A  R  Y  N  E  L  A  N  X
R  T  L  E  R  K  T  H  L  X  D  I  M
Y  M  I  P  L  R  H  Y  M  E  L  P  U
T  H  E  E  T  H  I  C  K  E  T  E  D
X  D  A  R  L  I  N  G  H  J  E  S  D
L  M  E  O  P  M  G  Z  P  A  R  T  Y
```

SING-ALONG

One of the Ingalls family's favorite activities was singing. So grab a family member or a friend and sing this song beloved by Laura and her family!

"Polly-Wolly-Doddle"

"When Pa had agreed that he and Laura could buy an organ for Mary, he said: "By jinks! I feel like celebrating. Bring me my fiddle, Half-Pint, and we'll have a little music."

VERSE 1:

Oh, I went down South for to see my Sal,
Sing polly-wolly-doodle all the day;
My Sally was a spunky gal,
Sing polly-wolly-doodle all the day.

Farewell, farewell, farewell, my fairy fay,
For I'm off to Louisiana for to see my Susy Anna
Singing polly-wolly-doodle all the day.

VERSE 2:

Oh, my Sal she is a maiden fair,
Sing polly-wolly-doodle all the day;
With curly eyes and laughing hair,
Sing polly-wolly-doodle all the day.

CHORUS

HIDE THE THIMBLE
GAME

During the dark and cold days of winter, Laura and Mary could not stay outside for long. So they played all kinds of games indoors, including Hide the Thimble. A thimble is a little metal cup that fits on top of your finger when you're sewing. It keeps the needle from hurting your fingertip as you push the needle through the fabric.

To play Hide the Thimble, you will need:
- A thimble (or other small object)
- One or more friends

1. Choose who will hide the thimble first.
2. All the other players close their eyes and count to ten slowly while the thimble hider finds a good spot to hide the thimble.
3. Then the players open their eyes and look for the thimble, while the hider counts to fifty.
4. The first person to find the thimble is the one to hide it next. If no one can find the thimble in time, the same thimble hider hides it again, in a new place.

RECIPE:
TOWN PARTY LEMONADE

"Is your lemonade sweet enough?" Mrs. Oleson asked. So Laura knew that it was lemonade in the glasses. She had never tasted anything like it."

Now you can make your own Town Party Lemonade! To make lemonade, you will need:

1 CUP SUGAR   3 LEMONS
1 CUP BOILING   3 CUPS COLD WATER
   WATER   ICE

MEASURING CUP	SHARP KNIFE
SMALL BOWL	BOWL OR JUICER
LONG-HANDLED	PITCHER
SPOON	6 TALL GLASSES

1. Put the sugar into the small bowl and add the boiling water; stir to dissolve the sugar. Set aside.
2. Roll the lemons on a kitchen counter or table with your palm a few times to make them juicier.
3. Carefully cut the lemons in half.
4. Squeeze as much of the juice from the lemons as you can into a bowl, or use a juicer if you have one. Remove any seeds with a spoon.
5. Pour the juice into the pitcher.
6. Stir the sugar water into the lemon juice, then add the cold water and stir.

7. Taste the lemonade to see if it's sweet enough. If it isn't, add more sugar to taste.
8. Pour the lemonade over ice in tall glasses to serve.

This recipe serves six.

Laura and her sisters may live in a little house, but they're always ready for big adventure. Don't miss:

Chapter 1
CHRISTMAS IN THE BIG WOODS

Christmas was coming to the Big Woods of Wisconsin, where Laura lived with her Pa and Ma, her older sister Mary, and her baby sister Carrie. Their little log house was almost buried in snow. In the morning when Pa opened the door, there was a wall of snow as high as Laura's head.

The days were clear and bright, but it was too cold to play outside. Laura and Mary stood on chairs and looked out the window.

Great big icicles hung from the roof of the little log house. The icicles were as fat as the top of Laura's arm. The sunlight made them shine like glass.

At the end of every day, Pa came in from the cold with white frost on his mustache and beard. He stamped the snow from his boots and caught Laura up in a bear's hug against his big, cold coat.

Every night, Pa was busy. He was making a Christmas present for Ma.

Pa took one big piece of wood and two small pieces and whittled them with his knife. He rubbed them with sandpaper and with the palm of his hand. When Laura touched them, they felt soft and smooth as silk.

Then Pa took his knife and carved beautiful shapes into the pieces of wood. He cut holes in the shapes of windows, little stars, moons, and circles. All around them he carved tiny leaves and flowers and birds. When he was finished carving, he put all the pieces of wood together.

Pa had made a shelf for Ma. He hung it carefully on the log wall between the two windows. Ma placed her little china woman on the shelf.

The little china woman had a china bonnet on her head. China curls hung against her china neck. She wore a pale-pink china apron over her china dress. And she wore little golden china shoes. She looked beautiful standing on the shelf Pa had made.

Every day, Ma was busy too. She was making good things to eat for Christmas. She baked bread and Swedish crackers. She cooked a huge pan of baked beans with salt pork and molasses. She made pies, and she filled a big jar with cookies. She let Laura and Mary lick the cake spoon.

One morning Ma boiled molasses and sugar together until they made a thick syrup. Pa brought in two pans of clean, white snow from outdoors. Laura and Mary each had a pan. Pa and Ma showed them how to pour the dark syrup in little streams onto the snow.

Laura and Mary made circles, and curlicues, and squiggledy things with the dark syrup. The shapes became hard and were candy. Ma said that Laura and Mary could eat one piece each. The rest must be saved for Christmas.

Ma was doing all this cooking because Aunt Eliza and Uncle Peter and the cousins, Peter and Alice and Ella, were coming for Christmas.

Laura couldn't wait to see her cousins. She always played with Mary because Mary was her big sister and Carrie was too little to play with yet. And her cousins lived too far away to visit every day.

Laura liked playing with Mary most of the time. But Mary liked to play quiet games, and Laura liked to run and jump and shout. Laura's cousins liked to run and jump and shout too.

Chapter 2
THE COUSINS

The day before Christmas, the cousins arrived.

Laura and Mary heard sleigh bells ringing outside. The sound grew louder every minute. They looked out the window and saw a big bobsled come out of the woods and drive up to the gate.

Aunt Eliza and Uncle Peter and the cousins were in the bobsled, all covered up under blankets and robes and buffalo skins.

They were wrapped in so many coats and shawls that they looked like big, shapeless bundles.

When they came inside, the little log house was full. The cat ran out and hid in the barn. Jack, the bulldog, leaped in circles through the snow. He barked and barked as though he would never stop. Now there were cousins to play with!

As soon as Aunt Eliza had unwrapped the cousins, Peter and Alice and Ella and Laura began to run and jump and shout all at once. Even Mary, who was always so good, couldn't help jumping and shouting too. At last Aunt Eliza told them to be quiet.

"I'll tell you what we can do," Alice said. "Let's make pictures."

Alice said they must go out in the snow to make pictures. Ma thought it was too cold for Laura to play outside. But when Ma saw how sad Laura was, she said she could go for a little while.

Ma put on Laura's coat and mittens and the warm cape with the hood. Then she wrapped a scarf around Laura's neck.

When they were outside, Alice showed them what to do.

Alice climbed up on a tree stump. Then all at once she held her arms out wide and fell flat on her face into the soft, deep snow. Slowly and carefully she stood up and pointed to the ground. The shape in the snow looked exactly like a little girl. Laura and Mary clapped their hands in delight.

All day they played at making snow pictures. Laura had never had so much fun.

They played so hard that when night came, they were too excited to sleep. But they had to sleep, or Santa Claus would not come. So they hung their stockings by the fireplace and said their prayers and went to bed.

Alice and Ella and Mary and Laura all slept in one big bed on the floor. Peter slept on the little trundle bed. Aunt Eliza and Uncle Peter were going to sleep in the big bed. Another bed was made on the attic floor for Pa and Ma.

The buffalo robes and all the blankets had been brought in from Uncle Peter's sled, so there were enough covers for everybody.

The little log house had never been so full. Laura and the cousins tried to fall asleep, but they could not. They were wide awake, listening to the grown-ups tell stories by the fire.

Finally, Ma said quietly, "Charles, those children never will get to sleep unless you play for them." So Pa got his fiddle.

The room was still and warm and full of firelight. Laura could see Ma's shadow and

Aunt Eliza's and Uncle Peter's against the walls. Pa's fiddle sang merrily to itself.

Laura went to sleep listening to Pa and his fiddle sing softly.

The definitive full-color guide to the Little House series

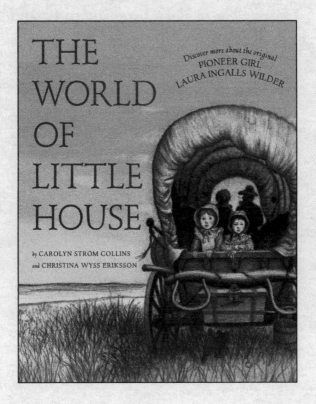

THE WORLD OF LITTLE HOUSE

Discover more about the original PIONEER GIRL LAURA INGALLS WILDER

by CAROLYN STROM COLLINS *and* CHRISTINA WYSS ERIKSSON

Featuring authentic photographs, maps, crafts, and recipes and a detailed exploration of how each of the beloved Little House books is connected to Laura's own pioneer days

HARPER
An Imprint of HarperCollinsPublishers

www.littlehousebooks.com

Little House for Younger Readers

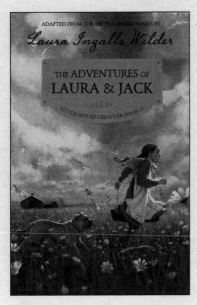

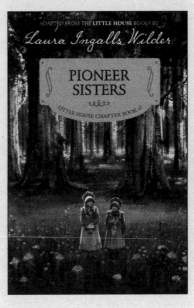

Grand adventures await in the Little House chapter books, adapted from Laura Ingalls Wilder's beloved classics

HARPER

An Imprint of HarperCollinsPublishers

www.littlehousebooks.com